*Christian Financial Concepts*
**Resourceful Living Series**
presents

*Larry Burkett's*

# Money in Marriage: A Biblical Approach

*A Six-Week Bible Study For Married or Engaged Couples*

All Scripture quotations in this book are from the New American Standard Bible, © 1960, 1962, 1963, 1968, 1971, 1972, 1973, 1975, and 1977 by The Lockman Foundation, and are used by permission.

Written by Larry Burkett with Michael E. Taylor
Managing Editor for Christian Financial Concepts: Adeline Griffith
Graphic design and layout: E. Chris Carey
Cover design: The Puckett Group


Library of Congress Cataloging in Publication Data

    Burkett, Larry
      Money in marriage.

      1. Finance, Personal—Religious aspects—
Christianity. I. Title.
HG179.B837     1982     332.024 82-7904

ISBN 0-8024-4230-7             AACR2


3 5 7 9 11 13 15 17 19 20 18 16 14 12 10 8 6 4


Printed in the United States of America

# Money in Marriage: A Biblical Approach

Congratulations on your decision to participate in the **Money in Marriage: A Biblical Approach** study. By faithfully completing the exercises and assignments, I believe you will take significant strides toward both finding fulfillment in your marriage and growing as a faithful steward in God's sight.

Over the last quarter of a century I have counseled literally hundreds of couples with financial problems. Although the exact details vary from one couple to the next, frequently the same spiritual issues surface. Money management is a spiritual task and, as a result, requires spiritual solutions. I believe the Bible has an answer for every problem you'll ever face—financial or otherwise. Too often people mistakenly believe that the only solution is more money. Rather, Jesus teaches that we must first live faithfully with what we already have before He will bless with more resources (Luke 16:10).

The apostle Paul reminds us of God's provision for our needs this way:

> "My God shall supply all your needs according to His riches in glory in Christ Jesus" (Philippians 4:19).

God faithfully supplies all that we need, and our responsibility is to faithfully live within our means and use the resources to glorify Him (see 2 Corinthians 5:15). To discover God's best for your marriage, you must first commit to living for Him.

**Money in Marriage: A Biblical Approach** is designed to help you live faithfully for Jesus Christ. You'll learn to organize your finances and increase your communication with key insights from your personality strengths and struggles. I'll answer some of the most common questions asked by couples who come for financial counseling. You'll also find a balance between biblical principles and practical life applications.

May God bless you abundantly as you complete the study materials and accept the challenge of making a difference for Jesus Christ in this strategic generation!

# *Money in Marriage: A Biblical Approach*

## *Table of Contents*

# An Overview of the Bible Study

Participants in the *"Money in Marriage: A Biblical Approach"* Bible study will be exposed to the following resources.

- ■ Six weeks of studies to review the fundamental biblical principles of managing money in marriage.

- ■ All the financial forms necessary to create a family budget, contained on the **CD-ROM** supplement in the back of this workbook.

- ■ Practical tips for reducing housing, automobile, and credit card debt.

- ■ A Life Pathways® *Personality I.D.*® inventory on **CD-ROM** that reveals how your personality impacts your money management tendencies.

- ■ How and why to become active members of a church family.

- ■ Bible verse memory cards and daily assignments.

This Bible study can be used by a couple or in a small-group setting.

# The *Six* Biblical Principles of
# MONEY IN MARRIAGE: A BIBLICAL APPROACH

**Principle #1:** Money management reflects your core values and thus serves as an accurate window to intimacy.

> **Biblical truth:** *"Where your treasure is, there will your heart be also"* (Matthew 6:21).

**Principle #2:** Your God-given personality tendencies impact your approach to money management.

> **Biblical truth:** *"I will give thanks to Thee, for I am fearfully and wonderfully made; wonderful are Thy works, and my soul knows it very well"* (Psalm 139:14).

**Principle #3:** Confidence in God eliminates the need for either hoarding or overspending in the Christian life.

> **Biblical truth:** *"Instruct those who are rich in this present world not to be conceited or to fix their hope on the uncertainty of riches, but on God, who richly supplies us with all things to enjoy. Instruct them to do good, to be rich in good works, to be generous, and ready to share"* (1 Timothy 6:17-18).

**Principle #4:** Accurate accounting of all assets and liabilities is a key step to financial freedom.

> **Biblical truth:** *"Know well the condition of your flocks, and pay attention to your herds"* (Proverbs 27:23).

**Principle #5:** Establishing a budget enables you to live according to God's priorities.

> **Biblical truth:** *"The plans of the diligent lead surely to advantage, but everyone who is hasty comes surely to poverty"* (Proverbs 21:5).

**Principle #6:** Church membership provides a supportive environment in which all aspects of stewardship can flourish.

> **Biblical truth:** *"Now God has placed the members, each one of them, in the body, just as He desired"* (1 Corinthians 12:18).

## Chapter One

# Finances:
# A Window to Intimacy

# Finances: A Window to Intimacy

### Chapter One Daily Studies

**Biblical Principle:** Money management reflects your core values and thus serves as an accurate window to intimacy.

> **Memory Verse**
> *"Where your treasure is, there will your heart be also"* (Matthew 6:21).

### Weekly Overview

Intimacy is the capacity to know, and be known, by another person. In the context of marriage, intimacy includes all dimensions of our humanity: intellectual, emotional, physical, and spiritual. This notion is captured in Genesis 2:25: *"The man and his wife were both naked and were not ashamed."* They had nothing to hide from one another.

Marriage presents the challenge of getting to know one another and learning to become one. Jesus taught that you could really get to know people by observing their patterns of money management. *"Where your treasure is, there will your heart be also"* (Matthew 6:21). Your study material this week uses money management to help you become better acquainted with your fiancé or spouse.

| A Peek at the Week | | |
|---|---|---|
| *Daily Homework* | *Study Title* | *Time Investment* |
| Day 1 | A Window to Intimacy with God | 25 minutes |
| Day 2 | A Window to Life Values | 20 minutes |
| Day 3 | A Window to Your Family's Financial Heritage | 20 minutes |
| Day 4 | A Window to Practical Matters | 15 minutes |
| Day 5 | A Window to Understanding God's Will | 20 minutes |

**Day One Homework—A Window to Intimacy with God**

Few circumstances in life parallel the joy and anticipation of becoming married. It's no wonder, because marriage takes precedence over all human relationships, even the bonding between parent and child.

Yet one relationship must take priority over marriage: your relationship with God. He created marriage. He knows you better than you know yourself, and by following His principles you can maximize intimacy in your marriage.

Today's material will introduce you to three key insights about God's character, as well as some ways He intends to use money in your marriage.

*Insights on God's Character and Money*

1. **God delights in meeting your needs** (Philippians 4:19).
   *Check the statements below that apply to you.*

   ☐ I am concerned that we struggle to pay our bills.

   ☐ I have experienced God's faithfulness to me in the past, and I have His peace as I look to the future.

   ☐ Sometimes I confuse my wants and desires with what I really need, and the result is that I usually overspend.

   ☐ It troubles me that I don't know how we can pay for our vacation (or honeymoon).

   ☐ Sometimes I feel like God has forgotten what my needs are.

   ☐ My spouse has a strong faith in God's ability to meet our needs.

   ☐ In my heart, I believe God really wants to bless our family.

   a. Now read John 3:16 and Romans 8:32. According to these passages, how can you be sure that God desires for you to have the very best in life?

   b. What might happen if you doubt that God delights in meeting your needs? For instance, what happened to Adam and Eve in Genesis 3?

2. **God gives you the power to make wealth** (Deuteronomy 8:18).
*Check the statements that apply to you.*

☐ I harbor resentment if my boss fails to provide periodic raises.

☐ Since my boss is not a Christian, I'm not sure that God will work
through him or her.

☐ I believe that God is sovereign—always in control—and I trust Him to
provide the amount of wealth consistent for His plan for my life.

I hope you checked the third box. The Bible provides many instances of God
working through unbelieving kings and leaders to provide for the welfare of His
people. For that reason, there is no need to be embittered against the authorities that
God has raised over you (Romans 13:1).

3. **God calls people to various economic levels in life** (Proverbs 22:2). Most
wedding vows include each person vowing to remain faithful to one another "for
richer or for poorer."

a. What temptations could you face because of riches (Deuteronomy 8:11-14)?

_____

_____

b. What temptations could you face because of poverty (Proverbs 30:7-9)?

_____

_____

c. Read Psalm 16:5-6 and respond to the statement below.

---

*"I pledge to accept God's provision for my family with
peace and contentment, whether we are rich or poor."*

☐ **yes**          ☐ **no**          ☐ **not ready to decide**

---

*How God Uses Money in Marriage*

*Draw a line from the principle in the left column to the matching Scripture reference. Then place a check mark (   ) beside the most important way you believe God is using money in your marriage. God uses money in marriage to:*

1. Demonstrate His faithfulness.

2. Stimulate your prayer life.

3. Teach cooperation in marriage.

4. Cultivate self-control in you.

5. Clarify your life values.

6. Reveal your need of a Savior.

a. Matthew 7:7-8

b. Matthew 6:19-21

c. Philippians 4:19

d. Ephesians 5:21

e. Proverbs 25:28

f. 1 Timothy 6:10-11

### Day Two Homework—A Window to Life Values

Jesus taught, *"Where your treasure is, there will your heart be also"* (Matthew 6:21). As you and your spouse build your relationship, your patterns of money management will reveal a great deal about your values and priorities. Complete the three exercises below on your own, and then compare your responses. Conclude your study time by praying for God to strengthen your relationship with the insights you gain today.

1. *Directions:* Based on the way you handle money, evaluate yourself, using the following chart. Circle the number that best describes your behavior. Then place an "X" over the number that best describes your spouse. When you are finished, discuss your perceptions. In the example below, the person completing the chart believes that he or she is more of a risk-taker than his or her spouse and represented that with an "O." An "X" represents the spouse's typical behavior.

| Trait | Example | Trait |
|---|---|---|
| Risk-taker | 1 (2) 3 4 X | Cautious |

Note: The correct matches are 1) c, 2) a, 3) d, 4) e, 5) b, 6) f

| Trait | Now you do it! | | | | | Trait |
|---|---|---|---|---|---|---|
| Risk-taker | 1 | 2 | 3 | 4 | 5 | Cautious |
| Planner | 1 | 2 | 3 | 4 | 5 | Impromptu |
| Cooperative | 1 | 2 | 3 | 4 | 5 | Stubborn |
| Humble | 1 | 2 | 3 | 4 | 5 | Prideful |
| Organized | 1 | 2 | 3 | 4 | 5 | Disorganized |
| Generous | 1 | 2 | 3 | 4 | 5 | Selfish |
| Decision-maker | 1 | 2 | 3 | 4 | 5 | Conforming |
| Patient | 1 | 2 | 3 | 4 | 5 | Impatient |

2. Suppose the two of you receive a surprise gift of $10,000 from a rich uncle. Working separately, outline a plan of what you would do with the money. Then compare your plans, but be careful to explore the values underlying your plans. How were your plans alike? different? _____

_____

_____

_____

3. How well do you know your spouse's financial habits? Mark the statements below true or false.

__a. My spouse and I seldom disagree on how to spend money.

__b. Both my spouse and I currently live on a budget.

__c. My spouse insists that we pay the bills on time.

__d. I know how much outstanding credit card debt my spouse has, if any.

__e. My spouse is committed to living on a budget.

__f. I have seen a current copy of my spouse's credit report.

__g. My spouse is completely honest in financial matters, including paying taxes.

4. In light of your exercises and discussions today, what particular financial skills about your spouse do you appreciate the most? _____

_____

_____

_____

_____

### Day Three Homework—A Window to Your Family's Financial Heritage

Parents have a remarkable influence over children, both good and bad. Perhaps you've adopted financial habits from one of your parents, or you may have chosen to manage your money differently than your parents did. Either way, the family you grew up with has helped to shape your money management habits. Today's material is designed to help you discover some of those influences and share them with your spouse.

1. Check the choices that describe where you learned the most about handling personal finances.

☐ Mom                    ☐ Relative

☐ Dad                    ☐ School

☐ Both parents           ☐ Learned on my own

☐ Foster parents         ☐ Observed a friend

☐ Stepparent             ☐ Other _____

2. If possible, describe how financial decisions were made in your family.

_____

_____

_____

_____

3. Describe how your parents resolved differences of opinion over money. In what ways do you handle conflict similarly to your parents? differently? _____

_____

_____

_____

_____

4. How does your spouse typically handle a difference of opinion with you? ____

----

----

----

----

5. Read Ephesians 4:25-32 and list below each communication principle you find.

----

----

----

----

**Day Four Homework—A Window to Practical Matters**

Today's study material will help you organize the practical responsibilities of money management in your marriage.

1. Which one of you is primarily responsible for the following tasks? Write the name in the blank provided.

   a. Issue checks for the bills on time  _____

   b. Balance the checkbook  _____

   c. Mail or deliver payment for the bills  _____

   d. Keep the bills organized in one place  _____

   e. Maintain a file of important records  _____

   f. Maintain file of income tax information  _____

2. The apostle Paul stated that *"the husband is the head of the wife, as Christ also is the head of the church"* (Ephesians 5:23), meaning that the husband must take primary responsibility for family finances before God. He also stated *"Be subject to one another in the fear of Christ"* (Ephesians 5:21). Frequently women are more skillful with numbers and organization than men. Explain your understanding of leadership in the home in the space below, and how you plan to maximize one another's God-given talents in your money management. _____

----

----

----

----

3. On a scale of 1 to 5, *where 1 is very important and 5 is not important at all,* circle the number that represents how important the practical financial task is to you. Then place an "X" over the number that, in your estimation, represents how important the task is to your spouse.

| Financial task | Degree of Importance |
| --- | --- |
| | *1 = very high — 5 = not important at all* |
| Establish a credit history | 1   2   3   4   5 |
| Balance the checkbook | 1   2   3   4   5 |
| Keep good credit records | 1   2   3   4   5 |
| Save as a lifestyle | 1   2   3   4   5 |
| Open credit card accounts | 1   2   3   4   5 |
| Keep three months income in reserve | 1   2   3   4   5 |
| Pay credit cards in full each month | 1   2   3   4   5 |
| Tithe (give 10 percent) to God's work | 1   2   3   4   5 |

### Day Five Homework—A Window to Understanding God's Will

There are more than 1,000 references to money in the Bible, second thematically only to love. Though not exhaustive, today's information is designed to lead you to an understanding of key insights for managing money, based on God's Word. Study each passage below and summarize the main points in your own words.

| Scripture Reference | Main Points in My Own Words |
| --- | --- |
| Malachi 3:10-11 | |
| Psalm 37:21 | |
| Proverbs 6:1-5 | |

*(Note: surety is borrowing without a certain way of repaying.)*

| | |
|---|---|
| Proverbs 6:6-8 | |
| Philippians 4:19 | |
| Proverbs 15:16-17 | |
| Hebrews 13:15 | |
| 1 Timothy 6:17-19 | |

Think back over all the exercises and discussions you completed this week. What new insights did you gain about yourself, your spouse, and God? List the three most important insights below. Then recite your memory verse, pray together, and give thanks for your growth in intimacy with God and one another.

**1.**

**2.**

**3.**

## Chapter Two

# Personalities...
# Plus Money!

# *Personalities...Plus Money!*

### *Chapter Two Daily Studies*

**Biblical Principle:** Your God-given personality tendencies impact your approach to money management.

---

**Memory Verse**

*"I will give thanks to Thee, for I am fearfully and wonderfully made; wonderful are Thy works, and my soul knows it very well"* (Psalm 139:14).

---

### Weekly Overview

This week's material will help you to discover the unique way that God has created your personality style and its impact on money management. You'll discover the same information about your spouse and learn to complement one another's strengths and struggles. Begin by taking the **Personality I.D.**® survey today and interpreting the results. During the balance of the week, you'll discover how your personality strengths and struggles impact the dimensions of your behavior:

- How you typically operate
- How you interact with others, including your spouse
- Insights regarding your approach to managing money.

---

### A Peek at the Week

| Daily Homework | Study Title | Time Investment |
|---|---|---|
| Day 1 | Complete the *Personality I.D.* Survey | 60 minutes |
| Day 2 | The Directing and Adapting Dimensions | 30 minutes |
| Day 3 | The Interacting and Reserved Dimensions | 30 minutes |
| Day 4 | The Supportive and Objective Dimensions | 30 minutes |
| Day 5 | The Conscientious and Unconventional Dimensions | 30 minutes |

**Day One Homework—Complete the Personality I.D.® Survey**

Today's assignment begins by completing the *Personality I.D.* survey on the CD-ROM enclosed at the back of this workbook. Before you begin the survey, read the five points below.

1. Complete your *Personality I.D.* surveys separately. Do not let your spouse help you answer. Load the CD-ROM and follow the directions on the screen.

2. When you have finished your survey, follow the directions to print your report.

3. When both of you have finished printing your reports, follow the directions on the screen to print the *Personality I.D.* Comparison Report.

4. When you finish with this software, you should have three printed reports: your own, your spouse's, and the *Personality I.D.* Comparison Report.

5. Take the survey now.

### Introduction to Personality I.D. Concepts and Charts

*Temperament* describes the unique blend of personality characteristics and motivations given to you by God. Some people are naturally more sociable and people-oriented; others are more shy. Some people naturally dwell on defining goals and accomplishing tasks; some tend to help and support others in practical ways.

Picture your temperament as the cruise control on your automobile. When you are operating naturally within the strengths of your temperament, certain tendencies result in your approach to life. In no way does this suggest that people are like robots who mechanically move at the impulse of some inner control system. In fact, under the leadership of the Holy Spirit, temperaments freely bring great honor and glory to God.

We have included a temperament survey (the *Personality I.D.*) in this study because blended temperaments operate uniquely, including how they manage money. By understanding your temperament more clearly, you will gain more insight into how and why you handle money like you do. In addition, you may find that your communication skills with your spouse will be enhanced.

*Assumptions of the* Personality I.D. *Survey*

In order to maximize your understanding of the *Personality I.D.* survey, there are several key concepts to understand.

1. **We are all born with certain differences in personality** and, thus, are motivated differently by circumstances, opportunities, and environments.

2. **God has designed us with these differences in motivation** so we can perform various functions at home, at work, and throughout our lives.

3. **Being different does not mean being wrong**; therefore, we should accept and respect people with different personalities. It is not our role to change others from the way God made them.

4. **All profiles/people have strengths and struggles.** Profiles should not be used as excuses to ignore bad habits or character flaws.

5. **By understanding our personalities, as well as how others are different, we are equipped to better manage our own lives** and live more effectively with others.

6. **There is no particular "best" temperament.** Rather, the goal is to discover how God has uniquely created you and others to glorify Him with a Spirit-filled temperament. Utilizing the knowledge of your personality strengths and struggles cannot be a substitute for maintaining a vital relationship with the Lord Jesus Christ.

7. **People are typically more successful when they operate from their strengths.** Learn what yours are and use them.

8. **When pushed to an extreme, strengths can become struggles** in daily living.

*Steps to Interpreting Your Reports*

1. The four dimensions of personality surveyed in *Personality I.D.* appear at the top of your report's first page. Your personal results appear as a solid line on the graph on the first page.

2. Your personal profile is graphed for comparison with the *closest matching* blended profile of typical temperament styles. The report describes various aspects of behavior that commonly occur with the blended profile. The closer your scores are to those of the blended profile, the more "on target" your description will be.

3. The farther your numbers plot to the extreme left and right sides of the graph, the more pronounced is that particular dimension in your personality style. For instance, a score of 50 (in the middle) indicates this dimension is mid-range behavior for you. A score of 30 or 70, however, indicates personality traits that are much more influential in daily behavior.

4. The subsequent pages of your personal report offer detailed insights into the personality strengths and struggles of the style most closely resembling your own. Carefully read this information and confirm the accuracy of the report by underlining or circling the key words and phrases that are particularly accurate.

5. Once your spouse has reviewed his or her report, turn your attention to the *Personality I.D.* Comparison Report. This document combines each of your graphs onto a single graph and offers a detailed discussion of how your strengths and struggles compare.

6. During the next four days, you will concentrate on understanding each of the four behavior dimensions (one each day) that are surveyed and measured by the *Personality I.D.* The goal is to understand yourself and your spouse better, as well as how your temperaments impact the way you manage money.

### Day Two Homework—The Directing and Adapting Dimensions

For each of the next four days, refer to your own *Personality I.D.* report that you printed.

1. Read the **Directing and Adapting** portion of your personal report, and summarize your strengths and struggles in the left column below. Prioritize the most accurate characteristics, and list the four most obvious ones below. Then, using your spouse's *Personality I.D.* report, summarize his or her strengths and struggles in the right column below.

| *Directing and Adapting Dimensions* | |
| --- | --- |
| Your strengths | Your spouse's struggles |
| | |
| *(Draw a line where you see a **strength** you have that compensates for a **struggle** your spouse has.)* | |
| Your struggles | Your spouse's strengths |
| | |
| *(Draw a line where you see a **strength** your spouse has that compensates for a **struggle** you have.)* | |

2. Read the Scripture verses to discover how the **Directing and Adapting** behavior dimensions can be seen in Jesus.

    a. Directing—John 2:13–16. What *Directing* characteristics do you see in Jesus?

    _____

    _____

    b. Adapting—John 19:7–11. What *Adapting* characteristics do you see in Jesus?

    _____

    _____

3. Both you and your spouse have personality characteristics just like Jesus. How does this truth change your willingness to be critical or disrespectful to one another in marriage? _____

_____

_____

4. Study the "Money Management Tendencies" portion in each of your reports (you and your spouse). Identify the unique contributions each of you make to family money management and discuss the struggle areas you can pray about together.

### Day Three Homework—The Interacting and Reserved Dimensions

1. Read the **Interacting and Reserved** portion of your personal report and summarize your strengths and struggles in the left column below. Prioritize the most accurate characteristics and list the four most obvious ones below. Then, using your spouse's *Personality I.D.* report, summarize his or her strengths and struggles in the right column.

## Interacting and Reserved Dimensions

| Your strengths | Your spouse's struggles |
|---|---|
| | |

*(Draw a line where you see a **strength** you have that compensates for a **struggle** your spouse has.)*

| Your struggles | Your spouse's strengths |
|---|---|
| | |

*(Draw a line where you see a **strength** your spouse has that compensates for a **struggle** you have.)*

2. Read the Scripture verses to discover the **Interacting and Reserved** behavior dimensions in Jesus.

a. Interacting—Matthew 5:1–2. What *Interacting* characteristics do you see in Jesus? _____
_____
_____

b. Reserved—Matthew 14:22–23. What *Reserved* characteristics do you see in Jesus? _____
_____
_____

3. It has been said, "Before marriage, opposites attract; after marriage, opposites attack." How do you think God can work through opposite characteristics, such as **Interacting and Reserved**, to make a stronger marriage? _____
_____
_____
_____

4. What impact do you suspect these personality characteristics (**Interacting and Reserved**) will have on your spending patterns in marriage? _____
_____
_____
_____

### Day Four Homework—The Supportive and Objective Dimensions

1. Read the **Supportive and Objective** portion of your personal report and summarize your strengths and struggles in the left column on the next page. Prioritize the most accurate characteristics, and list the four most obvious ones. Then, using your spouse's *Personality I.D.* report, summarize his or her strengths and struggles in the right column.

2. Read the Scripture verses to discover the **Supportive and Objective** behavior dimensions in Jesus.

a. Supportive—Matthew 9:35–38. What *Supportive* characteristics do you see in Jesus? _____
_____
_____
_____

---

## Supportive and Objective Dimensions

| Your strengths | Your spouse's struggles |
|---|---|
| | |

*(Draw a line where you see a **strength** you have that compensates for a **struggle** your spouse has.)*

| Your struggles | Your spouse's strengths |
|---|---|
| | |

*(Draw a line where you see a **strength** your spouse has that compensates for a **struggle** you have.)*

---

b. Objective—Matthew 19:16-26. What *Objective* characteristics do you see in Jesus? _____
_____
_____

3. In what ways could family finances suffer if the *Supportive* characteristics are carried to the extreme? What if the *Objective* characteristics are carried to the extreme? _____
_____
_____

4. How can these personality characteristics (**Supportive and Objective**) make a positive contribution to maintaining financial records from month to month? _____
_____
_____
_____

### Day Five Homework—The Conscientious and Unconventional Dimensions

1. Read through the **Conscientious and Unconventional** portion of your personal report and summarize your strengths and struggles in the left column on the next page. Prioritize the most accurate characteristics, and list the four most obvious ones. Then, using your spouse's *Personality I.D.* report, summarize his or her strengths and struggles in the right column.

---

### *Conscientious and Unconventional Dimensions*

| Your strengths | Your spouse's struggles |
|---|---|
|  |  |

*(Draw a line where you see a **strength** you have that compensates for a **struggle** your spouse has.)*

| Your struggles | Your spouse's strengths |
|---|---|
|  |  |

*(Draw a line where you see a **strength** your spouse has that compensates for a **struggle** you have.)*

---

2. Read the Scripture verses to discover the **Conscientious and Unconventional** behavior dimensions in Jesus.

    a. Conscientious—Matthew 5:48–6:18. What *Conscientious* characteristics do you see in Jesus? _____

_____

_____

    b. Unconventional—Mark 6:30–44. What *Unconventional* characteristics do you see in Jesus? _____

_____

_____

3. What strengths do each of these dimensions (**Conscientious and Unconventional**) offer to the process of successfully resolving conflict? _____

_____

_____

## Case Study

When Don and Sue completed reading their **Personality I.D.** reports, problems ensued. Sue scored high in the **Conscientious** dimension, and indeed she was a natural with numbers; she could balance the checkbook and keep up with the details. Don was just the opposite; he scored strongly in the **Unconventional** dimension. Yet, as a new Christian husband, he took seriously the biblical admonition to function as the head of his household (Ephesians 5:23). How can Don and Sue be faithful to biblical truth as well as to their God-given temperament strengths? What advice can you offer to them?

My advice to Don and Sue is _____

_____

_____

_____

_____

_____

_____

_____

_____

_____

_____

_____

_____

_____

_____

_____

Think back over all the exercises and discussions you completed this week. What new insights did you gain about yourself, your spouse, and God? List the three most important insights below. Then recite your memory verse, pray together, and give thanks for your growth in intimacy with God and one another.

**1.**

**2.**

**3.**

Chapter Three

# Hoarding or Overspending: Discovering Your Money Management Tendencies

.

# Hoarding or Overspending: Discovering Your Money Management Tendencies

### Chapter Three Daily Studies

**Biblical Principle:** Confidence in God eliminates the need for either hoarding or overspending in the Christian life.

> ### Memory Verse
> *"Instruct those who are rich in this present world not to be conceited or to fix their hope on the uncertainty of riches, but on God, who richly supplies us with all things to enjoy. Instruct them to do good, to be rich in good works, to be generous and ready to share"* (1 Timothy 6:17–18).

### Weekly Overview

Not only does personality influence money management; our spiritual condition does too. Two of the most common symptoms of spiritual immaturity are hoarding and overspending. Both conditions fail to reflect the balance and maturity God desires. When an overspender marries a hoarder, the stage is set for conflict. Left unresolved, Satan can use this stress as a wedge to divide husbands and wives.

This week offers an inventory that is designed to reveal your tendencies toward hoarding or overspending, as well as a review of key biblical passages for correction. The goal is to avoid hoarding or overspending, because they lead to pain and heartache.

| A Peek at the Week | | |
|---|---|---|
| *Daily Homework* | *Study Title* | *Time Investment* |
| Day 1 | Complete the Inventory | 30 minutes |
| Day 2 | The Solution to Hoarding | 20 minutes |
| Day 3 | The Solution to Overspending | 20 minutes |
| Day 4 | Resisting Temptation | 20 minutes |
| Day 5 | Learning to Work As a Team | 30 minutes |

### Day One Homework—Complete the Inventory

Insert your CD-ROM and open the "Hoarding or Overspending" file. Follow the directions, print the results, and summarize them below.

**Husband's tendencies** _____ **Wife's tendencies** _____

If your tendency is to hoard, answer questions 1 and 2 below. If your tendency is to overspend, answer questions 3 and 4.

1. **Hoarding** is accumulating material goods and money far above and beyond what is required for basic needs. In fact, legitimate family needs may be overlooked or neglected when a person has this tendency. People who hoard may sometimes be described as tight, stingy, frugal, cheap, or miserly. Look around your home. Do you see obvious signs of hoarding? Does your spouse detect any? _____

_____

_____

_____

_____

2. How does a firm confidence in God alleviate the need for hoarding? _____

_____

_____

_____

_____

3. **Overspending** is the opposite extreme and means habitually spending more money than is available. The inability to say "no" to the latest new electronic gadget, toy, or sale at the mall makes the overspender easy prey in today's world of advertising. Look around your home. Do you see obvious signs of overspending? Does your spouse detect any? _____

_____

_____

_____

_____

4. How does a firm confidence in God alleviate the desire for overspending? ___

_____

_____

_____

_____

### Day Two Homework—The Solution to Hoarding

Today's material covers the spiritual causes and solutions of hoarding.

1. Read Philippians 2:5-7. How is hoarding unlike Jesus Christ? _____
   _____
   _____

   a. Read Philippians 2:6. Let your imagination roam by naming some of the resources to which Jesus had access while in heaven. If you need help with ideas, read Revelation 5:12-13. _____
   _____
   _____

   b. Read Philippians 2:7. In what ways would your life be different if Jesus had chosen to hoard all His resources and privileges and remain safely in heaven?
   _____
   _____

2. *"Have this attitude in yourselves which was also in Christ Jesus"* (Philippians 2:5). What may happen if you continue to hoard things or money?

*Check all that apply if you hoard resources.*

☐ I likely won't be stretched in my faith and may miss even more blessings God intends for me.

☐ I likely won't experience the joy of giving to others.

☐ The needs of other people may remain unmet.

☐ I may experience bondage to things.

☐ My family may not see Christ in me as clearly.

☐ I may fail to see God's faithfulness and provision in my life.

☐ I may get to the end of my life with many material possessions but realize I've missed my real purpose.

☐ Other: _____

3. *"You will be enriched in everything for all liberality, which through us is pro-*

*ducing thanksgiving to God"* (2 Corinthians 9:11).

*Check all that apply if you stop hoarding.*

☐ I may experience the joy of helping others in practical ways.

☐ I may find fulfillment of God's purpose in my life.

☐ I may see more clearly why God blesses me with abundant resources.

☐ God may entrust even more resources to me.

☐ My spouse and I may experience less tension over money and things.

☐ Our home will be less cluttered.

☐ I will be able to find more security in God than in things.

☐ Other: _____

4. Draw a line to match each Scripture verse below to the spiritual cause of hoarding it addresses.

| | | |
|---|---|---|
| a. | 1 Timothy 6:9-10 | (1) lack of contentment |
| b. | Luke 12:15 | (2) envy |
| c. | Psalm 73:2-3 | (3) fear |
| d. | Daniel 4:30 | (4) greed |
| e. | Psalm 27:1 | (5) ego |
| f. | Matthew 23:12 | (6) love of money |
| g. | Hebrews 13:5 | (7) pride |

5. If you struggle with hoarding, write a prayer in the space below that tells of your desire to change. If your spouse struggles with hoarding, express a prayer for him or her.

*Dear God,* *"A broken and a contrite heart, O God, Thou wilt not despise"* (Psalm 51:17).

*Note: The correct matches are: a.(6), b.(4), c.(2), d.(7), e.(3), f.(5), g.(1)*

### Day Three Homework—The Solution to Overspending

Today's material covers the spiritual causes and solutions to overspending.

1. Self-control is listed as a fruit of the Holy Spirit in Galatians 5:22-23. Why is the lack of self-control unlike Jesus Christ? _____
_____
_____
_____

2. Read 1 Corinthians 9:24-27.

a. Why is self-control essential to success as an athlete? For instance, what might happen if the athlete trained only when he or she felt up to it? _____
_____
_____
_____

b. *"Everyone who competes in the games exercises self-control"* (1 Corinthians 9:25). One of the meanings of exercise is "to subject to forms of practice or exertion in order to train, strengthen, or condition." Describe how you can exercise self-control while shopping at a mall. _____
_____
_____
_____

3. *"The rich rules over the poor, and the borrower becomes the lender's slave"* (Proverbs 22:7). In the following list, check all the consequences of overspending that apply.

☐ We will not be able to save money consistently.

☐ We will incur debt—maybe deep debt!

☐ My spouse may become very disappointed and discouraged with me.

☐ We may develop a bad credit record.

☐ I may become depressed because things will never satisfy my soul.

☐ We may file bankruptcy.

☐ We may be unable to purchase a home when we want.

☐ We may be unable to give to God's work as freely as we want.

☐ Other: _____

4. *"There is precious treasure and oil in the dwelling of the wise, but a foolish man swallows it up"* (Proverbs 21:20). In the following list, check all that may happen if you stop overspending.

☐ We may begin to save money consistently.

☐ As our savings grows, we will have more money available to meet unexpected repairs and needs.

☐ We will regain a sense of balance and control over our financial matters again.

☐ We will have resources to help others in a time of need.

☐ Our lives will be a testimony that God is sufficiently supplying our needs.

☐ We can build a good credit record more easily.

☐ We will experience less tension over finances in our marriage.

☐ Other: _____

5. Match each Scripture verse below to the spiritual cause of overspending it addresses.

| | |
|---|---|
| a. Ephesians 5:3 | (1) pride |
| b. Proverbs 25:28 | (2) greed |
| c. Deuteronomy 8:11-14 | (3) lust |
| d. Matthew 6:25-34 | (4) lack of self-control |
| e. 1 John 2:15-17 | (5) lack of contentment |
| f. Philippians 4:11-12 | (6) lack of faith |
| g. Psalm 37:1-6 | (7) anxiety |

6. If you struggle with overspending, write a prayer in the space below that tells God of your desire to change. If your spouse struggles with overspending, express a prayer for him or her.

*Dear God,* *"A broken and a contrite heart, O God, Thou wilt not despise"* (Psalm 51:17).

*The correct matches are: a.(2), b.(4), c.(1), d.(7), e.(3), f.(5), g.(6)*

### Day Four Homework—Resisting Temptation

Although hoarding and overspending are different extremes of managing money, both represent a temptation to act in a less-than-Christlike manner. Today's material will equip you to recognize and overcome temptation.

1. Recognize the sequence of temptation.

   a. Satan begins temptations with a lie. Read Genesis 3:1-4.

   (1) What lie did Satan tell in verse 1 (compare to Genesis 2:16)?

   (2) What lie did Satan tell in verse 4 (compare to Genesis 2:17)?

   (3) What lies from Satan encourage overspending and hoarding?

   *Check all that apply.*

   ☐ I will feel much better if I just buy this item.

   ☐ I will feel more secure with just a little more money in the bank.

   ☐ I can't live without this item.

   ☐ He who dies with the most toys wins.

   ☐ Money will alleviate my fears.

   ☐ I earned this money and I plan to spend it any way I choose.

   ☐ God isn't supplying my needs now, much less for the future. I have to hang on to all I can get.

   ☐ Sure I can afford this; I still have checks!

   ☐ Other:

   b. Fill in the blanks. *"But each one is tempted when he is _____ _____ and enticed by his own _____. Then when lust has _____, it gives birth to _____; and when sin is accomplished, it brings forth _____"* (James 1:14-15).

2. Seek deliverance from temptation.

   a. Experiencing temptation is not a sin; yielding to temptation is sin.

   *"No temptation has overtaken you but such as is common to man; and God is faithful, who will not allow you to be tempted beyond what you are able, but with the temptation will provide the way of escape also, that you may be able to endure it"* (1 Corinthians 10:13).

(1) According to this verse, is it unusual for you to be tempted to hoard or overspend? Why or why not? _____

_____

_____

(2) According to this verse, when you find yourself in the throes of temptation, what does God do? *Check one.*

☐ God becomes so thoroughly disgusted with me that He turns His back to me in shame.

☐ God is faithful to me and actively helps me to endure the temptation.

(3) In addition to being faithful, name two more actions God takes to help you endure the temptation.

☐ _____

☐ _____

b. God desires for you to experience victory over temptation.
   Personalize the verse below by writing your name in each blank.

*"Thanks be to God, who always leads _____ in His triumph in Christ, and manifests through _____ the sweet aroma of the knowledge of Him in every place. For _____ [is] a fragrance of Christ to God among those who are being saved and among those who are perishing"* (2 Corinthians 2:14–15).

c. God provides the power for you to overcome temptation.

(1) Read James 4:7–8. What must you do before you resist the devil? ____
_____ . Why is that step essential?

_____

_____

(2) According to Proverbs 18:10, to what is the name of the Lord compared? What is the result of obeying the action stated in the verse? _____

_____

_____

_____

### Day Five Homework—Learning to Work As a Team

You and your spouse no doubt bring a variety of differences to marriage. The *Personality I.D.* helped you to see differences in your personalities. In addition to overspending and hoarding tendencies, there are other differences: the *roles* between husband and wife, gender *perspectives*, socioeconomic *backgrounds,* and educational *experiences.* In fact, at some point you may become mildly alarmed at the number of differences the two of you have.

Not to worry. One of the mysteries of marriage is how beautifully God can weave two different lives into a pattern of unity that reflects His glory. There are two critical dimensions to achieving this unity: a *spiritual* dimension and a *practical* "what to do after we've prayed" dimension. Let's begin by examining spiritual unity between a husband and wife.

1. Every team has common elements: a leader; a clear mission or purpose; and vital contributions made by each member.

    a. Who is the essential leader in a Christian marriage?
(See Philippians 2:10-11.) _____

    What may happen if Jesus is not honored in marriage?

    *Check all that apply.*

    ☐ Two people may battle for control.

    ☐ One person becomes a dictator; the other seethes in silence.

    ☐ A positive Christian witness to neighbors and friends will be compromised.

    ☐ Children will grow up without Christian role models for parents; future generations will be negatively impacted.

    ☐ The couple will fail to receive the finest of God's blessings.

    b. What is the essential mission or purpose of Christian marriage? (See Colossians 3:17.) _____

    c. Read Ephesians 5:25. What was the one thing the apostle Paul commanded husbands to do? _____
What model was provided for husbands to fulfill this command?

    _____

    Husbands, ask your wives why this is so important to them. _____

    _____

    _____

d. Read Ephesians 5:33. What was the one thing the apostle Paul commanded wives to do? _____
Wives, ask your husbands why this is so important to them. _____
_____
_____

e. Although you cannot *make* your spouse love and serve Jesus Christ, wonderful things can happen in a marriage as each spouse grows closer to Christ and, as a result, closer to each other.

*By individually growing closer to Jesus Christ, the husband and wife naturally grow closer together. If people focus on each other instead of Jesus, they will inevitably find faults and shortcomings. The "big bang" that follows is no theory!*

2. As the two of you build a spiritual unity in Christ, you also can build unity in financial matters by committing to living on a budget. A budget is simply an organized plan for directing your expenditures. It helps you to make financial decisions, rather than yielding to mushrooming expenditures.

a. If you are married to an overspender, how can a budget help to curtail impulsive spending patterns? _____
_____
_____

b. If you are married to a hoarder, how can a budget help to loosen that person's grip on the family cash flow? _____
_____
_____

c. What is the *maximum* amount of money that either of you will spend without first checking with the other person? Write the amount here and place your initials beside it. $ _____    _____

# The Chatter Box

*Think back over all the exercises and discussions you completed this week. What new insights did you gain about yourself, your spouse, and God? List the three most important insights below. Then recite your memory verse, pray together, and give thanks for your growth in intimacy with God and one another.*

**1.**

**2.**

**3.**

Chapter Four

# *Financially: Where Are We?*

# *Financially: Where Are We?*

### *Chapter Four Daily Studies*

**Biblical Principle:** Accurate accounting of all assets and liabilities is a key step to financial freedom.

> **Memory Verse**
>
> *"Know well the condition of your flocks, and pay attention to your herds"* (Proverbs 27:23).

### *Weekly Overview*

When two people marry, they not only become intertwined emotionally, spiritually, and physically, but they also join their finances—both assets and debts. Do you know where you are financially? where your spouse is?

This week's material is designed to help you clarify one another's present financial condition by summarizing how much debt you have, as well as creating a statement of net worth. You'll discover one another's attitudes toward using credit, creating financial goals, making investments, and purchasing insurance. Overlooking these very topics frequently leads to staggering financial setbacks for many newlyweds. Your commitment to completing the homework this week will provide a solid foundation for managing money for years to come.

| **A Peek at the Week** | | |
|---|---|---|
| *Daily Homework* | *Study Title* | *Time Investment* |
| Day 1 | Getting the Facts in Focus | 30–60 minutes |
| Day 2 | Where Are We on Using Credit? | 20 minutes |
| Day 3 | Where Are We on Financial Goals? | 60 minutes |
| Day 4 | Where Are We on Investments? | 20 minutes |
| Day 5 | Where Are We on Insurance? | 15 minutes |

### Day One Homework—Getting the Facts in Focus

In biblical times, a measure of family wealth was the size of one's flocks and herds of animals—the more, the wealthier. In this week's memory verse, wise Solomon instructs you to know where you are financially—meaning, understand your assets and liabilities. In marriage, the two of you should accomplish this task together.

Your assignments below will require some research. For this reason, you may want to spread the work over several evenings. Don't delay in getting started!

1. Complete the "My List of Credit Card Debts" form at the end of this chapter. You will transfer the sum of your credit card accounts to the "Net Worth Statement" form mentioned below.

2. Complete the "Net Worth Statement" form at the end of this chapter; pay particular attention to the footnotes. Under liabilities, be sure to list every financial obligation you have, including student loans, vehicles, alimony, child support, and loans from family. If you owe it, list it. If you need more space, attach a separate piece of paper. An example is provided for you at the end of the chapter.

Note: If you are engaged, complete the forms individually and share the results. If you are already married, complete one set of forms.

### Day Two Homework—Where Are We on Using Credit?

"I'll gladly pay you Tuesday for a hamburger today," was the line that made Wimpy famous (he was a character from the Popeye cartoon series and comic strip). It reveals how using credit has become central to the fabric of American society. Where are you in your knowledge of biblical guidelines of using credit?

1. Determine whether each of the following statements is true or false. Use "T" to indicate "true," and "F" to indicate "false."

___ a. The Bible teaches that God's people sin if they borrow.

___ b. Christians are no longer obligated to repay debts if a bankruptcy court discharges the debts.

___ c. It is a sin for Christians to file for bankruptcy.

___ d. The Bible says you become a slave to the lender when you borrow.

\_\_\_ e. If you lend money to another Christian, the Bible says you are
not to charge interest.

\_\_\_ f.  The Bible says you can borrow only if you have a certain way to
repay.

\_\_\_ g. The Bible teaches you that it's no big deal to delay repaying
what you owe when you have the means to do it immediately.

\_\_\_ h. Since my credit record deals with monetary rather than spiritual
matters, it is of no concern to God.

*Answers:*

a. *False.* The Bible gives specific instruction on loaning to other people
(e.g., Exodus 22:25; Deuteronomy 15:6). God does not teach people to
sin. Rather, the Bible never speaks of borrowing in a positive light
and, instead, offers many cautions against borrowing. Although
borrowing is not a sin, it may not be a wise step.

b. *False.* Psalm 37:21 teaches that it is wicked to borrow and not pay
back. Even if human courts dissolve your debts, God says you are to
repay, regardless of how long it takes.

c. *False.* In some cases, creditors may unite to force you into
bankruptcy. Other times bankruptcy may be the only option to
ensure equitable distribution of your assets or perhaps even to
maintain mental health. Filing bankruptcy is not a sin; failing to
repay your obligations is (Ecclesiastes 5:4-5).

d. *True.* Proverbs 22:7 states that you relinquish some degree of
freedom when you incur debt.

e. *True.* Exodus 22:25 and Deuteronomy 23:19-20 teach that believers
offer a testimony by not charging interest to fellow believers—a
testimony that we are more committed to God than we are to the
loss of a little revenue.

f.  *True.* The biblical word is surety, and it means having a certain, or
sure, way to repay what you borrow. Proverbs 6:1-5 teaches you to
get out of surety just as quickly as possible.

g. *False.* Proverbs 3:27-28 teaches that you should repay promptly when
it is within your ability to do so.

h. False. Proverbs 22:1 and 1 Timothy 3:7 teach the value of
maintaining a good name and reputation in the community. Failing
to do so will likely compromise your witness for Christ.

2. What attitudes or habits, if any, do you plan to change in light of God's Word on using credit? _____

_____

_____

### Day Three Homework—Where Are We on Financial Goals?

*"If you don't know where you're going, any road will get you there!"* Similarly, if you don't create financial goals, you can't evaluate your financial progress.

In the years ahead you will face a variety of important financial decisions. Having financial goals will provide an important context for deciding what is the wisest and best action for you to take. Today's material will help you determine realistic financial goals for the next five years, as well as strategies to achieve those goals.

1. Read Luke 14:28-30 and Proverbs 21:5. Based on these verses, why it is a good idea to create financial goals? _____

_____

_____

2. A financial goal states an end result you plan to achieve. It must be firm enough to provide structure and direction to your financial efforts, yet flexible enough to allow for unexpected, dramatic changes in finances. Financial goals should be consistent with God's Word.

Examples include being free of all consumer debt, repaying a certain portion (if not all) of your student loans, building six months of your income into an emergency surplus account, saving 10 percent each month, tithing, or paying off your automobile loans.

Work together to formulate a list of financial goals for the next five years of marriage. Pray together and seek God's wisdom, and be patient since this activity will require much conversation and perhaps several attempts. When finished, share your goals with your parents, your pastor, or a married couple who could mentor you through this process.

Goal #1: _____

_____

_____

Goal #2: _____

Money in Marriage: A Biblical Approach

Chapter
Four

_____

_____

Goal #3: _____

_____

_____

Goal #4: _____

_____

_____

Goal #5: _____

_____

_____

Goal #6: _____

_____

_____

Goal #7: _____

_____

_____

Note: If you need more space, simply insert another piece of paper at this point.

3. Your next step is to develop strategies to meet your financial goals. Goals state what you plan to do; strategies state how you plan to do it. For instance, suppose you set a goal of having your cars completely paid off in five years. A strategy to help you meet that goal would be to plan to continue driving and repairing your current vehicles for the next five years. Or, you may elect to postpone purchasing a home until a certain amount of savings is reached or your credit cards are paid off. Another strategy could be to scale back your plans for vacations for the next couple of years.

Strategies define the lifestyle you intend to live in order to reach your financial goals. As in goal setting, plan to be firm but yet flexible. Continue to work together; use this space to state specific strategies that will help you reach your five-year goals.

Strategy #1: _____

_____

_____

Strategy #2: _____

_____

_____

_____

Strategy #3: _____

_____

_____

_____

Strategy #4: _____

_____

_____

_____

Strategy #5: _____

_____

_____

_____

Strategy #6: _____

_____

_____

_____

Strategy #7: _____

_____

_____

_____

Strategy #8: _____

_____

_____

_____

Note: If you need more space, simply insert another piece of paper at this point.

### Day Four Homework—Where Are We on Investments?

Trends reveal that Americans are waiting longer to get married. On occasion, this results in newlyweds who are more financially established than younger couples. Whether investing surplus funds is a concern for you now, it likely will be in your future. Today's material provides an overview of biblical principles of investing.

1. Match each biblical reference below to the investing principle it represents.

a. Ecclesiastes 11:2          (1) Seek godly counsel.

b. Proverbs 14:18          (2) Forsake a get-rich-quick attitude.

c. Proverbs 15:22          (3) God gives power to make wealth.

d. Hebrews 13:5          (4) Carefully evaluate risk and return.

e. Psalm 37:7          (5) Guard your heart from greed.

f. Luke 12:15          (6) Don't envy the wicked who prosper.

g. Deuteronomy 8:18          (7) Diversify your investments.

2. To invest means to spend resources to gain a future advantage or benefit, presumably at some degree of risk. A basic principle of investing is the greater the risk, the greater the potential return. Read Proverbs 28:20 and explain why making investments should be preceded by prayer and seeking wise counsel. _____

_____

_____

3. *"From everyone who has been given much shall much be required; and to whom they entrusted much, of him they will ask all the more"* (Luke 12:48). How does your marriage represent an investment to Jesus? For example, what is He depending on you to accomplish? _____

_____

_____

_____

4. Why is it shortsighted to sacrificially invest in the stock market when you still have credit card balances on which you are charged high interest rates? _____

_____

_____

_____

### Day Five Homework — Where Are We on Insurance?

An atmosphere of euphoria typically surrounds the months preceding and following a wedding. Yet there are very practical business elements involved in establishing a new household, and one of them is purchasing insurance. Where are you on

*The correct matches are a.(7), b.(4), c.(1), d.(2), e. (6), f.(5), g.(3)*

organizing your plans for insurance? To help you, some of the most common questions about insurance are addressed in today's material.

1. *Is insurance scriptural?* Although insurance is not specifically defined in Scripture, the concept can be found in these verses and others:

   a. 2 Corinthians 8:14–15—The apostle Paul teaches you to share with those in need out of your abundance in order that they may do likewise. Similarly, insurance claims are settled from premiums paid in advance by policyholders.

   b. Proverbs 22:3—King Solomon taught that wise living sees danger approaching and makes provision in advance. Life can be unpredictable, and insurance—regardless of the type—is designed to provide when a potential loss is catastrophic.

2. *What type of life insurance is best for you?* There are two basic types of life insurance available: *term* and *whole life*.

   a. Term—As its name suggests, term insurance lasts for a specified "term," meaning you are purchasing coverage for a specific window of time. Beyond that, you must reapply for new coverage. Term insurance is attractive because it is cheaper. There are two disadvantages, however. When the term expires, the insured must requalify for new coverage. And, the policy doesn't pay anything unless the insured person dies.

   b. Whole life — As its name suggests, whole life insurance is designed to provide coverage for your lifetime. It may also be called universal or permanent insurance. It is attractive because it builds cash value in addition to providing coverage. The downside is that it costs more than term insurance.

   *Check the statement that applies to you.*
   ☐ We have decided to purchase term life insurance.
   ☐ We have decided to purchase whole life insurance.
   ☐ We have decided to decline life insurance altogether.

3. *How much insurance should you purchase?* This question is difficult to answer because your family has a variety of variables to consider: the number and ages of children you have; current lifestyle; existing debt; and how much income, if any, would be available to a surviving spouse without life insurance.

A good starting point for discussion is this: What lump sum of money would need to be invested so that the surviving spouse could live off the interest? How much interest from the investment would be required to replace the annual income of the deceased? A general rule for calculating the proper amount of life insurance coverage is ten times the amount of the annual income being replaced.

---

**Use this formula to calculate the amount for you.**

**Your annual income:** $ _____
**(multiplied by ten)** x 10
**Life insurance needed:** $_____

---

4. There are a variety of other insurance coverages you should consider purchasing. *Place a check mark beside each coverage you have (or plan to purchase).*

- ☐ Disability insurance—This replaces a substantial portion of your income if you become unable to continue providing income for your family.

- ☐ Health insurance—This covers a substantial portion of medical and hospital bills.

- ☐ Automobile insurance—This is probably required in your state.

- ☐ Renter's insurance—Suppose you live in an apartment and the person living downstairs below you falls asleep while smoking and the place burns down. This insurance replaces your contents in a rental dwelling.

5. There is one final aspect of responsibly making provision for the future: making a will. You may be thinking, "I can't even *think* about living without my spouse. Besides, we're so young!" Just check the obituary page in your local newspaper; death is not limited to elderly people. Consider the following scenarios.

- a. Jay and Marcy both die in a head-on collision with a drunk driver, leaving three children as orphans. Without a will, the state courts determine who will raise the children, even if living relatives are willing to assume that responsibility. Would you want your children to be in this situation?
  ☐ *yes*   ☐ *no*

- b. Joe is a partner in running a small business. Following his accidental death on the job, the business goes broke. Without a will, his surviving wife Alice is faced with a legal nightmare of sorting out

business and personal liabilities, in addition to grieving for her departed husband. Would you want this to be your situation?
☐ *yes*  ☐ *no*

*Check the statement that best applies to you.*

☐ We already have a will.

☐ We agree that we need a will and plan to have one written.

☐ We plan to have a will, but we're procrastinating.

☐ We don't agree that we need a will.

Think back over all the exercises and discussions you completed this week. What new insights did you gain about yourself, your spouse, and God? List the three most important insights below. Then recite your memory verse, pray together, and give thanks for your growth in intimacy with God and one another.

**1.**

**2.**

**3.**

# Husband's List of Credit Card Debts

*(as of _____ )*

*"I can do all things through Him who strengthens me"* (Philippians 4:13).

| Creditor or Account | Contact Name Phone # | % Rate (APR) | Payoff Amount | Remaining Payments | Monthly Payment | Due Date |
|---|---|---|---|---|---|---|
| 1. | | | | | | |
| 2. | | | | | | |
| 3. | | | | | | |
| 4. | | | | | | |
| 5. | | | | | | |
| 6. | | | | | | |
| 7. | | | | | | |
| 8. | | | | | | |
| 9. | | | | | | |
| 10. | | | | | | |
| 11. | | | | | | |
| 12. | | | | | | |
| 13. | | | | | | |
| 14. | | | | | | |

*(Permission is granted to make and work from a photocopy of this page if you wish.)*

# Husband's Net Worth Statement

## Assets

### 1. Liquid assets

Total       $_____

### 2. Invested assets

Total       $_____

### 3. Use assets

Total       $_____

## Liabilities

### 4. *List accounts and balances*

Total       $_____

## Net Worth
(Assets minus liabilities)

Grand Total Assets   $_____

minus –

Total Liabilities      $_____

equals =

Net Worth        $_____

**Explanation of Terms:**
1. Liquid assets: cash, savings accounts, checking accounts.
2. Invested assets: IRAs, TSAs, 401(k)s, investment real estate, CDs, antiques presented at fair market value.
3. Use assets: residence, autos, personal belongings presented at fair market value.
4. All outstanding loans: real estate, auto, family, and student; alimony; child support; and credit card totals from the "List of Credit Card Debts" worksheet.

*(Permission is granted to make and work from a photocopy of this page if you wish.)*

# Wife's List of Credit Card Debts

*(as of _____)*

*"I can do all things through Him who strengthens me"* (Philippians 4:13).

| Creditor or Account | Contact Name Phone # | % Rate (APR) | Payoff Amount | Remaining Payments | Monthly Payment | Due Date |
|---|---|---|---|---|---|---|
| 1. | | | | | | |
| 2. | | | | | | |
| 3. | | | | | | |
| 4. | | | | | | |
| 5. | | | | | | |
| 6. | | | | | | |
| 7. | | | | | | |
| 8. | | | | | | |
| 9. | | | | | | |
| 10. | | | | | | |
| 11. | | | | | | |
| 12. | | | | | | |
| 13. | | | | | | |
| 14. | | | | | | |

*(Permission is granted to make and work from a photocopy of this page if you wish.)*

# Wife's Net Worth Statement

## Assets

### 1. Liquid assets

_____    _____
_____    _____
_____    _____
_____    _____
_____    _____
_____    _____
_____    _____

Total                    $_____

### 2. Invested assets

_____    _____
_____    _____
_____    _____
_____    _____
_____    _____
_____    _____
_____    _____

Total                    $_____

### 3. Use assets

_____    _____
_____    _____
_____    _____
_____    _____
_____    _____
_____    _____

Total                    $_____

## Liabilities

### 4. *List accounts and balances*

_____    _____
_____    _____
_____    _____
_____    _____
_____    _____
_____    _____
_____    _____
_____    _____
_____    _____
_____    _____
_____    _____
_____    _____
_____    _____
_____    _____
_____    _____
_____    _____

Total                    $_____

### Net Worth
(Assets minus liabilities)

Grand Total Assets   $_____
                minus –
Total Liabilities        $_____
                equals =
Net Worth               $_____

**Explanation of Terms:**
1. Liquid assets: cash, savings accounts, checking accounts.
2. Invested assets: IRAs, TSAs, 401(k)s, investment real estate, CDs, antiques presented at fair market value.
3. Use assets: residence, autos, personal belongings presented at fair market value.
4. All outstanding loans: real estate, auto, family, and student; alimony; child support; and credit card totals from the "List of Credit Card Debts" worksheet.

*(Permission is granted to make and work from a photocopy of this page if you wish.)*

# Net Worth Statement

## Assets

### 1. Liquid assets

| | |
|---|---|
| SAVINGS | $1,200 |
| CHECKING | $350 |

Total $ 1,550

### 2. Invested assets

| | |
|---|---|
| IRA | $3,500 |

Total $ 3,500

### 3. Use assets

| | |
|---|---|
| 1998 CAR | $14,000 |
| FURNITURE | $4,500 |
| HOUSE | $125,000 |

Total $ 143,500

## Liabilities

### 4. List accounts and balances

| | |
|---|---|
| VISA | $1,200 |
| AMEX | $350 |
| FURNITURE LOAN | $500 |
| 1998 CAR LOAN | $12,000 |
| HOME MORTGAGE | $115,000 |

Total $ 129,050

### Net Worth
(Assets minus liabilities)

Grand Total Assets $ 148,550

minus –

Total Liabilities $ 129,050

equals =

Net Worth $ 19,500

SAMPLE

**Explanation of Terms:**
1. Liquid assets: cash, savings accounts, checking accounts.
2. Invested assets: IRAs, TSAs, 401(k)s, investment real estate, CDs, antiques presented at fair market value.
3. Use assets: residence, autos, personal belongings presented at fair market value.
4. All outstanding loans: real estate, auto, family, and student; alimony; child support; and credit card totals from the "List of Credit Card Debts" worksheet.

## Chapter Five

# Creating Your
# First Budget

# Creating Your First Budget

## Chapter Five Daily Studies

**Biblical Principle:** Establishing a budget enables you to live according to God's priorities.

> ### Memory Verse
>
> *"The plans of the diligent lead surely to advantage, but everyone who is hasty comes surely to poverty"* (Proverbs 21:5).

## Weekly Overview

For some, budgeting is a breeze and will present no problems whatsoever. Others put budgeting right next to getting a root canal on their favorite-things-to-do list. And still other people are open to living on a budget but never were trained in financial matters by their parents or schools, and they simply don't know how to proceed.

This week's material will equip you to understand the process of budgeting, help you to create your first budget, and make the necessary adjustments to live on a budget in the future.

| A Peek at the Week | | |
|---|---|---|
| *Daily Homework* | *Study Title* | *Time Investment* |
| Day 1 | Budgeting: Grasping the Big Picture | 15 minutes |
| Day 2 | Practice Makes Perfect! | 45 minutes |
| Day 3 | Calculating Your First Budget | 60 minutes |
| Day 4 | Adjustments: How to Make Ends Meet | 30 minutes |
| Day 5 | Sticking to a Long-Term Commitment | 20 minutes |

### Day One Homework—Budgeting: Grasping the Big Picture

A budget is simply an organized plan for managing finances in order to meet your financial goals. The plan to manage money for a year is an *annual* budget, which, divided by twelve months, becomes your *monthly* budget.

By following a financial plan, you become empowered to control your finances under the lordship of Jesus Christ, rather than your finances dictating what you will and won't do. In short, budgeting leads to financial freedom—freedom *from* all the grief and heartache of financial floundering and the freedom *to* respond to God's prompting to do *what* pleases Him *when* He prompts you!

### 1. Comprehending the Process

It is critical that you understand the big picture of budgeting prior to working with actual numbers and financial forms. A budget simultaneously controls and regulates your expenditures in a coordinated fashion. This process—*controlling and regulating resources*—has a number of common parallels in American culture. Once you grasp the process of controlling and regulating, you'll be well on your way to understanding budgeting.

The example below captures the importance of controlling and regulating resources.

    a. *Hoover Dam* — Completed in 1936, Hoover Dam rises 726 feet over the floor of Black Canyon in Nevada. The monstrosity controls and regulates the flow of the Colorado River and yields the following benefits.

- The dam stops massive flooding of the Colorado River each spring.
- Lake Mead is created by the dam and yields year-round critical water supplies for the southwestern desert.
- Powerful turbines supply hydroelectric power for cities across the southwestern United States.

    (1) There are over 39,000 large dams in the world, including 5,500 in the United States, making them a very popular form of harnessing God's natural resources. How is a budget similar to the controlling and regulating functions of a dam?

Check the following statements with which you agree.

☐ A budget will enable me to save extra money, similar to the way a dam creates a lake of surplus water.

☐ A budget will help me monitor my cash flow. That way, if I'm spending too much I know what areas to cut back. In the same way, if a dam releases too much water, it simply closes down some of the water release gates.

☐ A budget provides a specific method of providing during times when money gets tight, much like a dam creates surplus water during arid summer weather.

☐ A budget will help me divert money to projects and priorities based on God's Word, much like a dam provides irrigation to parched farmlands.

(2)  Self-control is listed as a fruit of the Holy Spirit in Galatians 5:23. Suppose a large dam suddenly burst due to the incredible water pressure behind it. How would the result compare to a person who lives without self-control over his or her finances? _____

_____

_____

_____

_____

## 2. Achieving Your Financial Goals

In the game of football, making a first down is not the ultimate goal of the game; neither is scoring touchdowns. The ultimate goal is to win. In cooking, the ultimate goal is not simply mixing ingredients in a bowl; rather, mixing is a step toward serving a nutritious meal or yummy desert!

In managing money, living on a budget is not the ultimate goal; instead, a budget is simply a tool or strategy to help you reach your financial goals. Have the two of you agreed prayerfully on financial goals?

a. Check the financial goals that a budget will help you to accomplish.

☐ Pay our bills on time

☐ Systematically save money

☐ Control spending

☐ Spend according to biblical priorities

☐ Ensure provision for future needs

☐ Establish and maintain an excellent credit history

☐ Be a faithful steward for Jesus

☐ Pay off our student loans

☐ Use money as a tool to build unity in marriage

☐ Save for a down payment on our first house

☐ Pay off our car loans

☐ Establish a three- to six-months emergency surplus fund

### Day Two Homework—Practice Makes Perfect!

Yesterday you studied how a budget can help you control and regulate your financial resources in order to meet your financial goals. Today's material will provide you with the opportunity to put those ideas into practice.

Using the worksheets at the end of this chapter, create a mini-budget for the following three components of your overall family budget.

1. Your honeymoon or vacation

2. Birthdays and special gifts

3. Christmas gifts

Remember to be realistic in creating your mini-budgets. It's one thing to plan to *spend* lavishly on a gift or event and quite another to *pay* for it. The goal is to help you make plans that are affordable. When you complete your calculations, ask yourselves, "Can we realistically afford to do this?"

### Day Three Homework—Calculating Your First Budget

The majority of today's work will be done on your computer, using the budget file from your CD-ROM. Prior to opening that file, please read the following notes.

In order to establish a budget, you must have access to specific resources:

• Your annual income—obtain this from last year's tax forms

• A record of your typical expenses—review your checkbook and cash receipts

• An example of a balanced budget at your income level—supplied on the Christian Financial Concepts software.

But suppose you don't have a consistent income, because you work on a commission basis or are self-employed. Then simply review your annual income from the previous year and divide it by twelve to arrive at an average monthly income. Of course, if you project that your income will sway dramatically (either higher or lower) during the year, allow for this when you establish your numbers.

Open the budget file on your CD-ROM at this time and follow the directions to calculate your budget. Be sure to print a report of your final calculations.

### Day Four Homework—Adjustments: How to Make Ends Meet

Congratulations! With the completion of your software budgeting exercise yesterday, your initial budget has come into focus. This represents your financial plan to live within your expenses and to glorify God with your resources.

If you're like many couples, however, you may be troubled by some or all of the *red* figures that appeared on your computer screen, indicating overspending. Some of the most common categories are: Housing, Automobile, Insurance, and Debt Reduction.

Today's material assumes that you have some categories of overspending that you want to correct. That means not only reducing your expenses to less than your income but also tithing faithfully to God's work, paying your bills on time, and saving consistently. *This is the norm—not the exception—for Christian living.*

*Key Thoughts and Attitudes to Consider*

1. You cannot continue to overspend indefinitely, because eventually, you will run out of money and credit.

2. Ignoring a pattern of overspending will only compound the problem, not resolve it.

3. If you don't want to go into debt, don't borrow. If you don't want to go deeper into debt, don't borrow more.

4. Beware of the "we deserve this" mentality. Perhaps you do deserve it, but the truth may be that you can't afford it.

5. People seldom get into debt overnight. Getting out of debt will likely require a long-term commitment. Thus, ask God for wisdom to make long-term lifestyle changes, rather than to seek quick fixes.

6. Beware of an attitude that "if I give God 10 percent of my income, I can do whatever I please with the other 90 percent."

7. Beware of thinking that faithful tithing is an excuse for disobedience to God in other areas of your life.

*Which of these seven points poses the biggest challenge to you and why?*

_____

_____

_____

_____

*Steps You Can Take to Reduce Debt*

1. Seek God's help by committing your circumstances to Him in prayer. Summarize the principle that each verse below offers to a strategy of debt reduction.

   a. Zechariah 4:6 _____

   _____

   _____

   _____

   b. Matthew 19:26_____

   _____

   _____

2. Honor God with the tithe. According to Malachi 3:10-11, how does God intervene in the life of one who faithfully brings the tithe to Him?

   _____

   _____

3. Stop overspending. Circle the categories on your budget report that have red figures on your computer screen. As usual, the color red denotes danger, and these figures are the prime areas in which you must cut your expenses.

4. Liquidate small assets in an emergency. Consider having a yard sale to sell items you don't use regularly. This step will prove futile unless you stop charging and borrowing.

   a. Are you presently in a financial emergency that requires selling small assets to make ends meet?     ☐ yes  ☐ no

   b. If yes, have you resolved to stop using credit cards and borrowing money?     ☐ yes  ☐ no

5. Consider options that will increase your monthly cash flow. For instance, selling a car, giving up a vacation, or moving to a more

affordable home. One couple waited to marry until each had finished postgraduate studies, but by then they were over $150,000 in debt for student loans. As a result, they postponed having children and purchasing their dream home. By living a lifestyle well below what their income would support, they rapidly reduced their debt load. In the space below, state some changes you will consider to increase your cash flow.

```
_____

_____

_____

_____

_____

_____

_____
```

6. Seek help from trained Christian counselors. For help with budgeting questions, contact Christian Financial Concepts at 1-800-722-1976 to locate a trained volunteer counselor in your vicinity. Call the Consumer Credit Counseling Service in Atlanta, Georgia, at 1-888-771-HOPE for help in restructuring your debt payments. Frequently this organization is able to intervene with your creditors and negotiate lower monthly payments and reduced interest.

**Day Five Homework—Sticking to a Long-Term Commitment**

It's one thing to *begin* your married life on a budget; it's quite another thing to *maintain* your commitment to this lifestyle in the years that follow. Study the following passages to discover encouragement for maintaining your long-term commitments.

1. *Read Matthew 7:24–27.* What did the wise man and foolish man have in common? _____

_____

What difference distinguished the two? _____

_____

How does this truth apply to all you have learned about managing money? _____

_____

2. *Read 2 Corinthians 8:11* and tell how it relates to managing your money.

_____

_____

_____

_____

3. *Read 1 Peter 2:9-13.* What positive outcome may follow your godly lifestyle, including your faithfulness with money? _____

_____

_____

How does verse 12 specifically apply to money management? _____

_____

_____

# Creating Budget Goals

*(Place your initials beside each budget goal on which you both agree.)*

_____ We agree to live on a budget.
_____ We agree to balance our checkbook to the penny every month.
_____ We agree to create a goal to set aside three to six months' income for an emergency surplus fund.
_____ We agree to pay off balances on our credit cards or stop using them altogether.
_____ We agree to live within our means.
_____ We agree to save something every month.
_____ We agree to tithe to God's work.

Think back over all the exercises and discussions you completed this week. What new insights did you gain about yourself, your spouse, and God? List the three most important insights below. Then recite your memory verse, pray together, and give thanks for your growth in intimacy with God and one another.

**1.**

**2.**

**3.**

# Creating Our Vacation/Honeymoon Budget

Transportation—there and back                       $_____
(*gas, airfare, car rental, and so on*)

Lodging                                             $_____

Meals                                               $_____

Recreation                                          $_____
(*admission fees, entertainment, shopping*)

Clothing needed for the locale or event             $_____

Souvenirs                                           $_____

Miscellaneous                                       $_____

Total estimated vacation expenditures               $_____

Total ÷ 12 months = amount to save each month       $_____

# Creating Our Birthdays/Special Gifts Budget

**Name**                                    **Approximate Amount for Gifts**

_____    _____

_____    _____

_____    _____

_____    _____

_____    _____

_____    _____

_____    _____

_____    _____

_____    _____

_____    _____

_____    _____

_____    _____

_____    _____

_____    _____

_____    _____

_____    _____

_____    _____

_____    _____

**Estimated total for all gifts**                       $ _____

**Total ÷ 12 months = amount to save each month**       $ _____

(Permission is granted to make and work from a photocopy of this page if you wish.)

# Creating Our Christmas Budget

Name                                        Approximate Amount for Gifts

_____                    _____

_____                    _____

_____                    _____

_____                    _____

_____                    _____

_____                    _____

_____                    _____

_____                    _____

_____                    _____

_____                    _____

_____                    _____

_____                    _____

_____                    _____

_____                    _____

_____                    _____

_____                    _____

**Estimated total for all gifts**                          $ _____

**Total ÷ 12 months = amount to save each month**          $ _____

(Permission is granted to make and work from a photocopy of this page if you wish.)

# Chapter Six

# Finding a Church Home

# Finding a Church Home

*Chapter Six Daily Studies*

**Biblical Principle:** Church membership provides a supportive environment in which all aspects of stewardship can flourish.

> **Memory Verse**
> *"Now God has placed the members, each one of them, in the body, just as He desired"* (1 Corinthians 12:18).

## Weekly Overview

Without a doubt, the key to maximizing your joy and fulfillment in marriage rests in a relationship with Jesus Christ. After all, He not only created the two of you, He also created marriage!

To keep your relationship with Jesus Christ vital and growing, I heartily recommend your active participation in a church family. In church you can worship God, be challenged in your faith, fellowship with other couples of similar age, exercise your spiritual gifts, and function as salt and light in your community (see Matthew 5:13-16). The church offers the best setting for you to serve as a faithful steward of Jesus Christ.

This week's material is designed to assist you in finding and getting involved in a church family. In the event you're already established in a church family, the daily assignments will help clarify and solidify your involvement in the church.

### A Peek at the Week

| Daily Homework | Study Title | Time Investment |
|---|---|---|
| Day 1 | Reviewing Your Spiritual Heritage | 30 minutes |
| Day 2 | Finding a Church Home | 25 minutes |
| Day 3 | Giving to Your Church | 25 minutes |
| Day 4 | Making a Difference with Spiritual Gifts | 20 minutes |
| Day 5 | Reaching Out to Others | 25 minutes |

### *Day One Homework—Reviewing Your Spiritual Heritage*

One of the goals of both your engagement period and marriage is becoming better acquainted with one another's spiritual heritage. Every Christian has a story to tell about how and why he or she came to trust Jesus Christ as Lord and Savior. Reviewing your spiritual heritage also will help you to clarify where the two of you will be church members and serve Christ in the years ahead.

Today's material will help you review and discuss your spiritual heritage with your spouse. In addition to building spiritual intimacy with one another, investing this time will also prepare you for subsequent assignments later this week.

Use the chart on the following page to develop a timeline that reflects the following information.

- Specific dates and events surrounding your conversion to faith in Jesus Christ
- Specific times or events when you felt closest to God
- Specific people who have influenced you with their lifestyles or words
- Specific troubling events that challenged your faith in God
- Specific Scripture passages that were meaningful to you at each point

When finished, share the entries from your chart with your spouse.

### *Day Two Homework—Finding a Church Home*

Today's material will help you identify and discuss the factors that you believe are important to becoming established in a church family.

1. From the nine choices below, check the statement that applies best to you.
   - ☐ We attend church in the denomination in which I was raised.
   - ☐ We attend church in the denomination in which my spouse was raised.
   - ☐ We attend church in a different denomination from our backgrounds.
   - ☐ We haven't decided where to attend church.
   - ☐ Attending church is important to me but not to my spouse.
   - ☐ Attending church is important to my spouse but not to me.

*Money in Marriage: A Biblical Approach*

## Example of My Christian Heritage Timeline

1975 — BORN TO CHRISTIAN PARENTS WHO READ BIBLE STORIES AND TOOK ME TO FIRST COMMUNITY CHURCH.

YOUTH PASTOR JEFF EXPLAINED THE GOSPEL TO ME; TOLD ME THAT GOD HAD A PLAN FOR MY LIFE AND THAT GOD DESIRED A RESPONSE FROM ME; I BEGAN TO REALLY SEARCH THE SCRIPTURES.

1987 — FELT SUPER-CLOSE TO GOD AT THE SUMMER YOUTH CONVENTION AT THE BEACH; BEGAN HAVING MY OWN QUIET TIMES EACH MORNING!

I ACCEPTED CHRIST AS MY LORD AND SAVIOR; BAPTIZED IN MORNING SERVICE IN APRIL, 1988! KEY VERSES WERE JOHN 5:24; ROMANS 8:31-39.

1991 — BEST FRIEND DIED IN A TRAGIC CAR ACCIDENT; I REALLY STRUGGLED TO UNDERSTAND "WHY?"; REALLY THANKFUL FOR SALVATION AND GOD'S GIFT OF ETERNAL LIFE; JOHN 11:25-26.

1993 — REALLY EXPERIENCING GOD'S GUIDANCE ON SELECTING A COLLEGE; MET NEW FRIENDS THE FIRST YEAR AT SCHOOL; CAMPUS PASTOR NAMED RUSS GOT ME INVOLVED IN STUDENT DISCIPLE-SHIP GROUPS; I BEGAN WITNESSING TO OTHER STUDENTS IN THE DORM. ISAIAH 41:10 WAS A KEY!

1995 — GOD LED ME TO THE PERSON I PLAN TO MARRY AND SPEND THE REST OF MY LIFE WITH; WEDDING DATE SET; FILLED WITH PRAISE TO GOD FOR HIS GOODNESS TO US! (JAMES 1:17)

1997 — I WILL GRADUATE FROM COLLEGE NEXT MONTH; GETTING MARRIED IN TWO MONTHS; GOD HAS PROVIDED A NEW JOB AFTER GRADUATION; I CONTINUE TO TRUST GOD WITH THESE BIG DECISIONS.

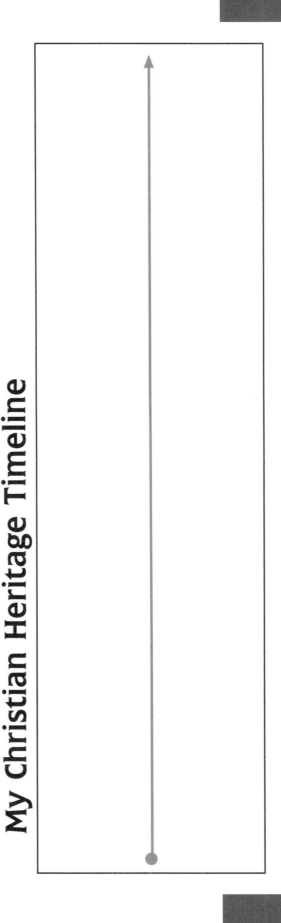

# My Christian Heritage Timeline

☐ We do not attend church at all.

☐ We joined the church in which we got married.

☐ Other _____.

2. Rate the aspects of church life below according to how important they are to you in choosing a suitable church family.

| Aspect of Church Life | Degree of Importance |
|---|---|
| | *1 = very high — 5 = not important at all* |
| Worship style | 1  2  3  4  5 |
| Relevant sermons | 1  2  3  4  5 |
| Fellowship with similar-aged couples | 1  2  3  4  5 |
| Opportunities to serve | 1  2  3  4  5 |
| Specific doctrines I believe | 1  2  3  4  5 |
| Where friends attend | 1  2  3  4  5 |
| Location to my home | 1  2  3  4  5 |
| Commitment to world missions | 1  2  3  4  5 |

3. Do you and your spouse have church backgrounds that are similar? In what ways are they alike? _____ _____ _____ _____ _____ _____ _____

4. If you come from different church backgrounds, what are some of the differences that you regard as significant? How do you plan to resolve these differences? _____ _____ _____ _____ _____ _____

5. Do you have specific doctrines that you regard as "essential" that determine the church you attend? If so, which? _____

_____

_____

_____

_____

_____

6. Paraphrase Hebrews 10:23-25. _____

_____

_____

_____

_____

_____

### Day Three Homework—Giving to Your Church

Active membership in your church provides you with a method of participating in a variety of ministries that you cannot accomplish on your own—ministries such as feeding the hungry, taking the Gospel to other nations, ministering to the homeless and orphans, teaching new Christians, and so on. If you can't perform the ministry personally, you can support those who carry on the work by sharing financially in the work of the church. Even more than supporting ministries, however, giving financially to your church is a responsible act of Christian worship!

Today's material offers a quick review of biblical references to tithes and offerings.

1. A tithe represents 10 percent of your income. According to Malachi 3:10-12, what did God challenge the people of Israel to do with their tithes? _____

_____

_____

What results would come from this obedience? _____

_____

_____

_____

2. According to Leviticus 27:32, what portion of your total increase does your tithe represent? _____

_____

_____

3. Read Haggai 1:3-14. According to verses 6, 9-11 of this chapter, what were some of the negative financial symptoms that the people of Israel were facing?

_____

_____

_____

a. In verses 4 and 9, what did God say was the root cause of these negative symptoms? _____

_____

_____

b. According to verses 12 to 14, how did the people of Israel remedy the situation? _____

_____

_____

c. How does this passage apply to your life? _____

_____

_____

_____

4. Study the Scripture passages below and summarize what important principle each passage teaches about giving to God's work.

a. Proverbs 3:9–10 _____

_____

_____

_____

b. 1 Corinthians 16:2 _____

_____

_____

_____

c. 2 Corinthians 8:1–5 _____

_____

_____

_____

d. 2 Corinthians 9:6–8 _____

_____

_____

_____

### Day Four Homework—Making a Difference with Spiritual Gifts

Today's material will focus on your calling not only to be a member of a church but also to serve effectively within that church. Study each passage below to discover God's desire to make a difference through your life and marriage.

1. God says we are part of the body of Christ.

   a. Read 1 Corinthians 12:12–27. In light of this teaching, what consequences do you see when Christians do not participate in the life of the church?_____

   _____

   _____

   _____

   b. Read Ephesians 4:11–16. What positive benefits will come from your participation in your church? _____

   _____

   _____

   _____

2. God has given us spiritual gifts to use in serving the church.

   a. Read 1 Peter 4:10. According to this passage, what are you to do with the gift God has given you? _____

   _____

   _____

   b. Do you know what your spiritual gift(s) is? _____

   _____

   _____

   If you don't know, ask your pastor for a spiritual gifts inventory to help you identify your gifts from God.

3. God will hold us accountable for the stewardship of the resources He has entrusted to us.

   a. 2 Corinthians 5:10 does not teach that the judgment seat of Christ is to determine whether we are really saved (see John 5:24 and 1 John 5:11-13). However, what is the result of standing individually before Jesus Christ? ___

   _____

   _____

   _____

   _____

   _____

b. Read 1 Corinthians 4:1-2. What is the one key trait God looks for from His people? _____

Does that word describe you? _____

How will this trait be apparent in your marriage? _____

_____

_____

_____

### Day Five Homework—Reaching Out to Others

Today's material will help you to look beyond your marriage relationship to the bigger picture of what God desires to accomplish by bringing the two of you together.

1. What did Jesus say to do in Matthew 28:18-20? _____

_____

_____

Do you believe you're included in the audience, or were His commands limited to only a particular group? _____

_____

2. Read Acts 1:8. In this verse, what did Jesus say we would receive from Him and what would be the result? _____

_____

_____

3. To what did the apostle Paul compare Christians in 2 Corinthians 2:14–16?

_____

_____

4. In the space below, name friends, family members, and coworkers who attended your wedding (or who will attend, if you're engaged) but who are not yet Christians. Then paraphrase Ephesians 1:16-19 to formulate a prayer for the people on your list.

a. Non-Christians at your wedding: _____

_____

_____

_____

_____

_____

b. Your prayer based on Ephesians 1:16-19:

## Dear God,

5. Was your wedding ceremony a Christian service (if you're engaged, will it be)? Check the elements that will specifically honor God during your ceremony.

☐ Prayers offered to God

☐ Christian message in the music

☐ Vows made in God's presence

☐ Ceremony held in a church

☐ Celebration of the Lord's Supper

☐ Gospel message presented by the pastor

☐ Unity candle explained

☐ Readings from God's Word

☐ Explanation of God's purposes for marriage

☐ Other _____

6. Check the statements below that best apply to you.

☐ Few of my friends know that I am a Christian.

☐ I pray consistently for my unsaved friends and family to accept Christ.

☐ We want our marriage to be a testimony to God's goodness and faithfulness.

☐ I want to share my faith with others, but I've never been trained how to do it.

☐ My spouse and I are considering serving God in another nation.

☐ Evangelism is a responsibility for older, more mature Christians—not me.

☐ I have helped at least one other person to accept Christ.

☐ I'm not sure what I believe about Jesus, so I wouldn't know how to help someone else believe in Him.

☐ I think our wedding ceremony is a strategic opportunity for friends and family to hear the message of Jesus Christ.

# The Chatter Box

*Think back over all the exercises and discussions you completed this week. What new insights did you gain about yourself, your spouse, and God? List the three most important insights below. Then recite your memory verse, pray together, and give thanks for your growth in intimacy with God and one another.*

**1.**

**2.**

**3.**

# Appendix A
## Questions for Larry Burkett

Answers to the following questions are found on your CD-ROM. Open the file, click on the question, and discover Larry's advice for you!

### Questions About Credit Cards

Q. Larry, credit card debt continues to mushroom in America. Do you recommend that couples avoid credit cards altogether? If not, under what conditions should they use them?

Q: Are there other precautions a couple can take to be sure that a credit card doesn't get out of hand?

Q: Many couples are eager to establish credit. How can they do that without getting into credit card debt?

### Are You Ready for Marriage? *(for engaged couples)*

Q: What advice do you have for the engaged couple planning to bring substantial debt into the marriage?

Q: Some engaged couples don't have serious debt, but neither do they have any savings. How important is this?

Q: What would you say to the couple that intends to marry but plan to keep separate bank accounts?

Q: Larry, you've spoken out against prenuptial agreements. Don't they provide a "safety valve" in case the marriage doesn't work out?

Q: Can a couple really "divorce-proof" their marriage?

*more...*

### Questions About Budgeting

Q: What are the most common problems couples face when they start budgeting?

Q: Speaking of housing, under what conditions should a couple consider purchasing their first home?

Q: How can a couple plan for the wife to stay home with the children?

Q: What should be a couple's first financial goal?

Q. Since the Bible describes the husband as the spiritual leader of the family, shouldn't he be the one to pay the bills?

### Questions About Financial Gifts

Q: It's not unusual for parents to want to help the newlyweds get started financially by offering gifts. Is this a good idea?

Q: Many couples make a very modest salary. If the parents can afford to help them buy a house or car, should they?

### Questions About Resolving Conflict

Q: Some parents have worked diligently to have assets to leave to their children. However, we understand that a wife having more assets than her husband can cause strife. Should that be an issue?

Q: Couples who have worked through this book will have a good understanding of how each of them views money. However, there will be times they disagree. What are your suggestions for resolving these conflicts biblically?

Q: Should every expenditure be discussed and agreed upon?

### Questions About Future Plans

Q: We know Scripture tells us that the two become one and that there is no age limit on this. However, when two people have assets from previous marriages, can something be set aside for each spouse's children?

Q: Larry, some Christians struggle with the issue of life insurance, believing that it is unscriptural and demonstrates a lack of faith in God. What advice do you have for couples on that topic?

Q: How can a couple pay off a house early?

Q: Thinking that they have their whole lives ahead of them and that they don't own much, many couples neglect to write a will. What's your advice to them?

### Miscellaneous Questions

Q: You recommend that pastors link newlyweds with older couples in the church. Why is that?

Q: Larry, early in the workbook you speak of finances functioning like a "window to intimacy." Why are finances such an important topic for couples?

# Appendix B
# Bible Memory Verses

**Money in Marriage: A Biblical Approach**
**Resourceful Living Series**

## Week #1

"Where your treasure is, there will your heart be also" (Matthew 6:21).

## Week #2

"I will give thanks to Thee, for I am fearfully and wonderfully made; wonderful are Thy works, and my soul knows it very well" (Psalm 139:14).

## Week #3

"Instruct those who are rich in this present world not to be conceited or to fix their hope on the uncertainty of riches, but on God, who richly supplies us with all things to enjoy. Instruct them to do good, to be rich in good works, to be generous and ready to share" (1 Timothy 6:17-18).

## Week #4

"Know well the condition of your flocks, and pay attention to your herds" (Proverbs 27:23).

## Week #5

"The plans of the diligent lead surely to advantage, but everyone who is hasty comes surely to poverty" (Proverbs 21:5).

## Week #6

"Now God has placed the members, each one of them, in the body, just as He desired" (1 Corinthians 12:18).

# Our Pledge to Faithful Stewardship

With God as our witness, we do hereby
pledge to live faithfully as stewards
in marriage, demonstrated in a
commitment to the following
principles of living.

1.  We resolve to live within the means that our Father God provides for us.

2.  We resolve to utilize our financial resources according to biblical principles.

3.  We resolve to be honest in every financial transaction, particularly when unfavorable to us at the moment, in order to glorify Jesus Christ.

4.  We hereby transfer the ownership of all of our material possessions to the Lord Jesus Christ, to be used for His purposes and His alone.


_____          _____
Husband                          Wife


Drafted the _____ day of _____,

in the year of our Lord and Savior Jesus Christ

_____.